this important manifestation of the community's potential strength in the international monetary sphere, however, its real interests were within the community itself ; and here, the ultimate aim of the common market (some form of political union) would be achieved using the vehicle of a common currency. Such a need was becoming somewhat imperative by the end of the 'sixties if the momentum within the community were not to be lost.

By the end of 1968, most of the major aims set out in the Treaty of Rome had been achieved. The death of de Gaulle, together with the insistence of some members of the common market that Britain should be admitted as a full member, underlined the urgent need for some kind of initiative. Thus it was that the heads of state of the six met in the Hague at the beginning of December 1969, and agreed, in principle, to achieve an economic and monetary union by 1980. Such a union would obviously imply the introduction and use of a common currency.

It is apparent that this support for a common currency reflects a desire for political integration in the EEC, in that it is believed a common currency will give an impetus to such integration. Member countries, in addition, want a common currency, or at least a fixed exchange rate system within the community, in order to have a commanding influence upon world monetary affairs and in order to put forward a unified personality in the international monetary arena (in particular there is now a common desire to provide a "solid" monetary front should a further dollar crisis occur). The reasons for this belief in the virtues of a common currency do not. however, rest there. France, in particular, regards a rigid exchange rate structure in the EEC as an essential condition for the successful operation of the Common Agricultural Policy (CAP). The adjustment of exchange rates within the community has a direct effect upon the common agricultural prices agreed between member countries. If a member country devalues its currency then its farmers have the advantage of receiving higher prices for their produce unless immediate action is taken. Furthermore, if higher prices persist, farmers may respond by increasing output, and this in turn may lead to a greater surplus of production than already exists in the community. These were the problems encountered after the French devaluation of August 1969, which brought pressures upon the Common Agricultural Policy. In the case of the revaluation of the mark, the opposite problems arose. Farmers in West Germany feared a fall in incomes. Again this placed heavy pressures upon the operation of the CAP. The solution agreed upon was that the agricultural fund and the West German government should share the burden of restoring farm incomes.

Undoubtedly a fixed exchange rate regime, or ultimately a common currency, is seen as providing some relief from these kinds of pressure upon the CAP. Indeed, the collapse of the common price system, which was the result of the dollar crisis which began in May 1971, has been a key factor in stimulating the new initiative towards monetary union ; particularly as the variable border tax, which was introduced to iron out changing exchange rates, and maintain common agricultural prices, has proven extremely difficult to operate. Last, but by no means of least importance, a common currency is viewed by most member countries as a stimulus to the further development of intra-community trade and the freedom of capital mobility. This, it is argued, is the result of the removal of uncertainty, and consequently the risks of trade, that exist where exchange rates are adjustable. It is also felt that the removal of the uncertainty involved in moving across national monetary frontiers may encourage an expansion of the number of multinational firms within the community.

the fundamental problems

Two questions have become the obsession of governments both within and without the European Economic Community. First, they wish to maintain the stability of their currencies, thus, in a number of cases, they tend to decide that the simplest manner of achieving this is to adopt fixed exchange rates. Such a policy, the protagonists maintain, also prevents governments from adopting wildly inflationary expansion policies. Even the many opponents of this policy cannot, therefore, throw it completely out of the window. Second, almost automatically stemming from the adoption of fixed exchange rates, there is the danger that socially and politically dangerous levels of unemployment might result from the self imposed discipline of deflation (in the classical sense, usually applied when the balance of payments runs into deficit, and possibly taking the form of increases in bank rate and credit restrictions and/or increases in taxation and/or cuts in government expenditure). The use of bank rate to attempt to restrict credit expansion in any one country of the community is particularly dangerous if undertaken at a time when the currency of that country is the object of speculative monetary inflows. The dual effect of changes in bank rate and speculative movements of currency tends to have a community wide inflationary effect.

The situation in Britain and West Germany in June 1972 was one of the best examples of the dangers of the application of outdated national monetary policies and the lack of a co-ordinated community policy. In West Germany a fairly strict internal monetary policy was being used at a moment when speculative inflows were continuing. (Nor should one ignore the fact that the *Bundesbank* felt forced to buy up huge quantities of dollars which tended to weaken the impact of the increased liquidity reserve requirements imposed on German commercial banks.) In the case of Britain, the outflows of money and the speculation against the pound encouraged the government to resort to an increase in bank rate. This, combined with the outflows of money, should have led to a scarcity of credit. Instead, the Bank of England came to the help of the commercial banks, and there was an increase rather than a diminution in the money supply. Thus, in the case of West Germany the money supply increased and the price of credit was unusually high, and in Britain the money supply remained high and the price of credit increased. In both countries an inflationary element was created and the fundamental speculation was not cured. The stability of exchange rates, the danger of unemployment, and the fact that the present and possible future members are still at different stages of economic development, have led to the development of two schools of economic thought within the community. "The monetarists" favour the swift imposition of fixed and equal exchange rates (that is, a common currency) with the national economic self discipline which such a policy implies, and "the economists" favour the prior careful co-ordination of the national economies before fixing exchange rates.

The over riding problem is that different nations are at different stages of economic development. In its most acute and obvious form, it takes the example of the industrial domination of West Germany, for whom the early adoption of fixed exchange rates might mean the importation of heavy inflation through the under pricing of her industrial goods ; and countries like France and Britain, who, needing to restructure their agriculture and industry, respectively, may through balance of payments difficulties be forced to deflate heavily, leading to high levels of unemployment. Here, part of the solution may lie in the provision of generous credits to nations facing such difficulties. However, the quality of the Treaty of Rome lies in its desire to guarantee a high standard of living to all members of the community. This means that the enrichment of any one nation at the expense of others should be avoided. When re-examining the experience of the 'twenties and 'thirties in Europe, one is fully aware of the catastrophic economic, political and social consequences of the acceptance of such a policy of the enrichment of one part of the community at the expense of the rest. However, other problems, which lie in the fundamentally different attitudes of national governments, are equally as serious ; for example, the heavy inflow of "hot money" into western Europe (particularly into West Germany) over the past year, the borrowing in the Eurodollar market, and the danger of disequilibriating movements of capital.

1. the meaning of monetary union

The successful removal of trade restrictions within the European Economic Community (EEC) has led its members to strive for even wider forms of integration in the community. The most far reaching integration proposed is that of monetary union, since it pre-supposes a movement towards political unification in the EEC. The ultimate objective of monetary union is to introduce a common currency. " A monetary union implies inside its boundaries the total and irreversible convertibility of currencies, the elimination of margins of fluctuation in exchange rates, the irrevocable fixing of parity rates and the complete liberation of movements of capital. It may be accompanied by the maintenance of national monetary symbols or the establishment of a sole community currency. From the technical point of view the choice between these two solutions may seem immaterial, but considerations of a psychological and political nature militate in favour of the adoption of a sole currency which would confirm the irreversibility of the venture." (*The Werner report,* English translation, page 10 of the supplement to bulletin 11 (1970) of the EEC.)

This monetary goal has met with a common acceptance by the existing members of the EEC. The means of achieving it, however, have provided the main source of dispute. It is in this dispute that the other features of monetary union come to the fore. Three extremely important features are distinguishable. The first is a desire to co-ordinate economic objectives and policy within the community. Here member countries are expected to agree upon common national objectives, particularly in relation to economic growth, price stability, and employment. Furthermore, they are expected to co-operate and consult with each other in deciding upon the necessary economic policy action to achieve these objectives ; in this way it is hoped that the policy action undertaken by one member country will not be inconsistent with, or limit, the efficacy of another member's policy action and *vice versa.* Second, there is a desire for some degree of fiscal harmonisation in the community, whereby similar types and rates of taxation would be applicable throughout the community. The principle example of this is obviously the value added tax (VAT). Third, the process of monetary integration seeks to bring about more freedom of capital movement within the community, by removing the obstacles to it (such as differential rates of taxation).

The dispute takes the form of the " monetarists," led by France, calling for the immediate implementation of irrevocably fixed exchange rates within the EEC, with strict controls over capital movements, and with economic co-ordination and harmonisation to follow at a later stage of integration, being opposed by the " economists," led by West Germany, who favour economic co-ordination before rigid exchange rates, and an early introduction of free capital mobility. In December 1969, the ministers of the six agreed, in principle, to achieve a complete economic and monetary union by the end of the present decade. (Article 8 of the final *communiqué* of the conference of the heads of state, The Hague, 1 and 2 December, 1969.) During the course of 1970, there followed a positive multitude of plans and agreements. (See appendix I, page 20, for the complete list.) This recent proliferation of studies and actions was in marked contrast to nearly twelve years of inactivity in the monetary sphere. Of these agreements, the principle ones are the agreements, made in June 1970, not to widen the existing margins round the parities of the EEC national currencies (candidates for membership would be invited to subscribe to this agreement), and the agreements made in Brussels in February 1971, and in March and October 1972.

This pamphlet reflects the bias of the authors. Both believe in European integration, but they also believe that it is impossible to impose a rigid time table for economic and monetary integration upon the enlarged European Economic Community. Further, great care must be taken to provide automatic help for nations who suffer from balance of payments deficits or whose currencies come under speculative pressure (for example, by the pooling of reserves). There is also an urgent need for a European regional fund which would be endowed with important resources. Such a fund should be heavily weighted in favour of depressed industrial areas since the Common Market Agricultural Fund is already responsible for agricultural areas. Moreover, the Europe of the 'seventies is not the United States of the nineteenth century and no national government could tolerate a situation which might, for example, lead to the setting up within the enlarged community of only one " Detroit " (the logical conclusion of an extreme specialisation and division of labour). Equally, a too rapid imposition of fixed exchange rates might result in potentially grave political, economic and social consequences. The community should, however, adopt a common attitude in the international monetary sphere. Since Britain will soon be a member of the EEC, she must use her influence to ensure that the accepted economic and monetary integration is undertaken with great care and that all necessary safeguards are provided before a common currency is introduced.

the arguments for monetary union

Economically powerful nations sooner or later produce strong currencies. Sometimes these monies become reserve currencies, and frequently such currencies are endowed with political influence. Such was the case with both the pound sterling and with the dollar. The real golden age of the pound sterling ended with the first world war, although we still are left with a legacy from that age. The dollar became powerful as a result of the second world war, and its supremacy was unquestioned until the early 'sixties when the United States started to experience a deficit on capital account and undertook excessive military expenditure abroad, which damaged the current account of the balance of payments. (The deficit on current commercial account is of relatively recent origin.) The decline of the dollar coincided with a resurgence of certain " hard " western European currencies, particularly the West German mark, the French franc, the Swiss franc and the Dutch guilder. The importance of these currencies was enhanced by the very important increase which was noted in the reserves of gold and foreign exchange of the countries of the European Economic Community (see table I below). As had previously been the case with Britain and the United States, it was perfectly reasonable that the common market countries should seek to weaken Anglo-Saxon hegemony in the international monetary sphere and to seek an international influence which corresponded more with their own economic strength. The first step in this direction was the demand, made by France in the mid-'sixties, that the United States should exchange some of her gold reserves for the dollars which France held in her reserves. The French also maintained that the unrestrained increase in dollars could only serve to destroy the whole international monetary system. The first major proof of the arrival of the currencies of the EEC countries on the world monetary stage was their ability, when the Special Drawing Rights (SDR's) were being set up, to ensure that reforms in the statutes of the International Monetary Fund (IMF) and in the future allocations of SDR's would require a majority of 85 per cent. This meant, in effect, that the common market countries would enjoy a right of veto in the fund. Apart from

TABLE I
GROSS RESERVES OF GOLD AND CONVERTIBLE CURRENCIES

period	EEC per cent	UK per cent	US per cent	total per cent
31 December, 1958	33.48	8.63	57.89	100.00
31 December, 1966	53.35	8.19	38.46	100.00
31 May, 1967	55.17	8.01	36.82	100.00

Source: statistical office of the EEC, *General statistical bulletin*, 1967, N.7-S.

2. various plans and agreements

Ministers in Brussels had a wealth of plans against which to make their decisions. (A thorough study of all these plans has been made by the authors in *European monetary integration,* Macmillan, November 1971.) However, the main plan to which they referred was the second Werner plan, published in Brussels on 8 October, 1970, which proposed specific details for the first stage of economic and monetary union which was to last from the beginning of 1971 until the end of 1973 (with a possibility of extending the period until the end of 1975). The importance of the second Werner plan lies in the fact that it is a compromise between the " monetarists " and the " economists." Its importance also lies in the detailed annex number 5, prepared by the Committee of the Governors of the Central Banks of the Member States of the EEC, in answer to a list of questions sent to the committee by Pierre Werner. In this section of Werner's report, the main consideration was that concerning the narrowing of the band around the parities of the community's national currencies. The ministers, having examined the report, met in Brussels in December 1970, when, although they agreed on the fundamental points regarding the implementation of the first phase of the economic and monetary union, they were unable to agree on a common attitude to the timing and degree of supra-national control which would eventually cover this union. So they met again in February 1971, and not only repeated their agreement of December 1970 about certain points, but also enlarged their horizons, thus deepening the spirit of compromise already obvious in the second report.

Brussels agreements

Basically, the initial phase of integration (that is, from 1971 to 1973 inclusive) was accepted, with the possibility of extending this until the end of 1975. (In view of the possibility of new members joining the community, this will almost certainly have to materialise.) It was agreed to narrow the bands around the parities of the EEC national currencies from 1.5 to 1.2 per cent (to come into effect on 15 June, 1971). In order to facilitate this task, a request was made to the relevant committees to prepare a report for June 1971 concerning the possibility of setting up, already during the first phase of integration, a European fund for monetary co-operation, which would act as a form of exchange equalisation account in maintaining the parities of the members' currencies within the agreed band. The third major decision was that concerning the co-ordination of national budgetary policies. To facilitate this task (and also to help the co-ordination of cyclical, fiscal, regional and monetary policies), the finance ministers will meet three times a year and will examine the national budgets before their presentation to the national parliaments. The ministers will follow the execution of the budgets. This means that the council of ministers will periodically examine reports from the member states on the application of the national budget and will ascertain whether the budget is being applied as originally laid down. Should there be a divergence from the original intentions, the council may make recommendations to the member government concerned. Of course, until now, the council has no means at its disposal of persuading member governments to keep to their original intentions.

These agreements had already been made, in principle, in Brussels in December 1970, and they are the fundamental points in the second Werner report. However, additional agreements were also made. First, the recommendation made by the commission in June 1970, regarding the provision of medium term credits to help members facing balance of payments difficulties was accepted. Second, the medium term economic plan was accepted, and third, it was agreed to examine the question of the provision of regional aid during the first phase of monetary integration. This last point is really very important and deserves complete support from the United Kingdom. Lastly, it was accepted that during the closing months of the first phase, that is towards the end of 1973, the commission would present a progress report to the council of ministers. The ministers would then be expected to decide on the moment of entering the second phase of integration. Here, they have the possibility of prolonging the initial phase for a further two years. A spirit of co-operation and compromise rather than an inflexible attitude of rapid and rigid interpretation has been a striking feature of these agreements. Possibly of very great importance is the fact that whilst changes in the parities of national currencies are to be discouraged (and the provision of medium term credits is a move in this direction), they are not, in the initial " extended " phase, excluded. Nevertheless, in this crucial initial phase, balance of payments considerations and regional problems become more important.

The importance of controlling borrowing from third parties has been particularly underlined in the case of West Germany. There, until the government agreed to discourage the practise, businessmen were quite free to borrow from the Euro-dollar market (where interest rates were most attractive), despite the fact that internally the government was attempting to apply a strict monetary policy. This example indicates that unless the community adopts a common attitude to borrowing from third parties, then one nation which allows its businessmen freedom to borrow where they wish, could sabotage the whole monetary management of the community through the inflow of large sums of money which would expand the community's credit creating base. There may obviously be occasions when a less rigid policy towards borrowing might be desirable, but again, if the EEC wishes to adopt a common monetary policy, the rules must be harmonised.

the "May events" 1971

During the weekend of 9 May the influx of dollars into West Germany, which had been substantial ever since the beginning of the year, reached astronomical proportions. (In 1970, the inflow of dollars accounted for a 23 per cent increase in the West German national money supply.) On one day alone (4 May) the *Bundesbank* had to buy up over 1,000 million dollars in order to maintain the dollar parity above the official floor. By the end of that week, the *Bundesbank* had been forced to cease its support for the dollar, and during the weekend of 8 and 9 May, the EEC ministers met to attempt to find a solution to the problem. The adoption of a common policy *vis-à-vis* the dollar was what was needed, and indeed the French were pressing for the adoption of common controls and the West Germans for a common floating of currencies. However, neither of these proposals were adopted. Instead, Holland and West Germany agreed to let their currencies " float," whilst Belgium allowed an official black market to materialise. Among the EFTA countries, Austria and Switzerland re-valued their currencies. In the banking sphere, both France and West Germany adopted the same policy. They both temporarily forbade the payment of interest on non-resident deposits held with their banks, and demanded that foreign currency holdings in their banks be backed by 100 per cent liquidity ratios. Later in the year Britain also forbade the payment of interest on non-resident deposits.

continuing crises

Enormous speculation against the dollar continued throughout the summer of 1971. On 15 August, President Nixon announced that the dollar would " float." In thus acting, the dollar became " inconvertible," and friendly central banks were left with large quantities of unusable dollars in their reserves. Richard Nixon also backed up his announcement with certain trade measures.

Following meetings by the EEC ministers, meetings of the group of ten in Paris, Brussels and Rome, in November and in December, and the meeting of President Pompidou with President Nixon in the Azores, the representatives of the group of ten met in Washington on 18 December, 1971. At this meeting certain agreements were made. Some of these (such as new parities for the main world currencies, and a wider band of 4.5 per cent for the dollar *vis-à-vis* other currencies) were effective. Others (such as, US agreement to a slight increase in the price of gold and to the removal of the 10 per cent surcharge which had been imposed on imports in August) were made in principle. There were other problems, however, which went unsolved; for example the very important question of the convertibility of the dollar was left unanswered. This poses very grave problems for the IMF and for those countries which owe this organisation money and which cannot settle their debts with their large holdings of dollars. The American deficit on current trade is of relatively recent origin and the percentage of her GNP which is composed of trade is quite small when compared with the members of the expanded European Economic Community.

Thus, in the long run, the devaluation of the dollar may, commercially, be rather difficult for the Europeans. It is probably the realisation of this fact which encouraged the common market to close its ranks and reach certain major agreements.

the agreements of February and March 1972

A compromise between the "economists" and the "monetarists," including the adoption of some common front to third party currencies, was absolutely essential if the proposed economic and monetary union were not to fall irrevocably into ruins. Thus, in February 1972, President Pompidou and Giscard d'Estaing met Chancellor Brandt and Professor Schiller in Paris. They reached the very important agreement to control short term capital movements between the EEC and third parties. Also, they agreed on inter-bank *concentration* throughout the community, to help currencies which might find themselves under speculative pressure. This would enable the currencies to remain within any band which might be chosen. These agreements paved the way for the very important agreements made in Brussels in March. Already on 6 and 7 March the finance ministers had met and reached certain agreements in principle. Two weeks later the agricultural, finance and foreign ministers met, and on 21 March certain crucial decisions were made public. First, it was agreed that the margins round EEC currencies should be reduced to 2.25 per cent. (It should be noted that this was really an experiment of an unlimited duration, see appendix 4.) In fact, the premature announcement of this decision had already had a practical psychological effect on the market because on 6 March the margin was 1.6 per cent, and on 19 March it was 2.08 per cent. In order to help members whose currencies might be under speculative pressure, and who would thus find difficulty in remaining within the agreed band, central banks would intervene, using, where possible, EEC currencies. The practical means of intervention are being worked out at the present moment. It is thought that settlements would be made between central banks at the end of every thirty days. In this field (and really following the advice contained in the fifth annex of the second Werner report), it should be noted that there already exists a "hot" line between all the EEC central banks, including the Bank of England.

Second, the commission's proposals, made on 23 June, 1971, regarding the control of movements of capital between the community and third parties were accepted. Member states agreed to enact legislation (if this had not already been done) enabling them to suspend interest payments on non-resident bank deposits and to discourage or prevent their nationals from borrowing from third parties.

Third, it was agreed to set up a high level economic co-ordination committee, composed of one important personality from each of the nine member states, together with one representative from the commission, which would meet in a free, open, informal and unrecorded manner on at least three occasions each year. In this framework, it was agreed that there should be a progressive development of a European capital market. Also it was agreed that there should be a harmonisation of indirect but not of direct taxes.

Fourth, in conformity with the demands made by Italy, some attention was paid to regional problems. It was agreed that the Common Market Agricultural Fund (FEOGA) would allocate 50 million units of account per annum for five years to industrial developments in depressed rural areas. Italy would, however, like to see a special and well endowed regional fund set up. Since the United Kingdom has regional problems (industrial ones mainly, it is true) of a similar dimension to those of Italy, it is to be hoped that, once we are members of an enlarged common market, we shall support Italy in her demands.

Lastly, as a result of intra-bank co-operation, it was not felt necessary to create a European reserve fund at the present time. This decision is somewhat debatable since the present strength of the EEC currencies is partly a result of the weakness of the dollar. When the dollar becomes stronger, however, the need for such a fund may be more obvious.

British decisions

Almost simultaneously with the decisions made in Brussels, Antony Barber announced a major relaxation of British exchange controls. The voluntary controls agreed upon by developed Commonwealth countries regarding their access to the London capital market were lifted. British companies were henceforth able to make direct investments of up to one million pounds in EEC countries, without going through the dollar premium ; previously this had been £250,000 or 50 per cent of the cost, whichever was the larger. Third, all restrictions were lifted on foreign companies borrowing in this country to invest in development areas. Finally, companies in the enlarged common market were enabled to borrow sterling on the United Kingdom market without restriction.

These decisions seemed somewhat premature, partly because there was no indication of how the agreements would work in practice, and partly because speculation might take place against a currency even when the balance of payments was in surplus (this did in fact happen in the case of Belgium in 1971). Further, there appeared a seeming incomprehension in British financial circles regarding the real implications of the decisions by the central banks of the community's member states to intervene in favour of each other's currency as the necessity should arise. Most observers saw in this agreement the germs of another European payments union (which had a large element of credit built into it). Unfortunately most observers failed to understand that accounts between central banks had to be settled at the end of each month. Thus should the franc come under pressure and should the pound sterling be favoured then the *Banque de France* would have to sell all the pounds sterling at its disposal and the Bank of England would buy up all the French francs it could ; but, at the end of each month the accounts would have to be settled. What would happen if the *Banque de France* ran out of reserves of foreign currency ? The enlarged community should pool its reserves or at least accord the same privilege as it gives to the dollar, that is, by buying up seemingly endless quantities of that currency until some settlement be negotiated in the future.

However, what had to happen did happen. Despite the fact that the reserves of gold and foreign currency held by the United Kingdom were really quite substantial (see table II below), speculation

TABLE II
GOLD AND FOREIGN CURRENCY RESERVES HELD BY THE UK

in millions of pounds	1967	1968	1969	1970	1971	1972 (April)
foreign exchange reserves	1,123	1,009	1,053	1,178	2,526	2,737
official short and medium term debts	2,067	3,363	2,664	1,369	415	—

started to take place against the pound sterling in mid-June and the central banks of the enlarged community were intervening to maintain the pound sterling within its band as from 15 June. The Bank of England was similarly intervening by buying up sterling as it came on the market.

However, such was the volume of speculation that on 22 June the bank rate (in a last attempt to hold back outflows of " hot " money) was raised from 5 to 6 per cent. Had the process continued in this manner, British foreign currency reserves would have been lost. Thus, only three months after the agreements of March 1972, the pound sterling was, as from 23 June, allowed to float against other currencies; and during the same weekend the treasury re-imposed controls on UK investment in the sterling area.

European repercussions

The pound sterling was not the only community currency to be under pressure, for the Italian lira was showing great weakness throughout June 1972. The partial relief given to the pound sterling placed additional pressure on the Italian currency. The combined difficulties of the two currencies led to the meeting of the community finance ministers in Luxembourg on 26 June when special help was organised for Italy. (In the case of the United Kingdom, the cost of intervention in June was about $3,009.) At this meeting France again stressed the need to set up a fund to help member countries who were facing difficulties similar to those encountered by Britain and Italy. Throughout this period, heavy pressure continued against the dollar and during two days alone, in the first week of July, the West German federal bank had to buy up $600 million. The Swiss adopted an 8 per cent levy on deposits of " hot " dollars. The West German federal bank asked commercial banks not to sell foreign securities to non-residents (in an attempt to restrict the utilisation of Euro-Deutschemarks and foreign loans in West Germany). Also, finally, the banks were asked not to organise loans in foreign currencies for their customers.

Again, in early July, the central banks had to intervene to save the dollar. The *Banque de France* bought 150 millions, the Swiss central bank 400 millions, the Dutch central bank 78 millions, the Belgians 20 millions and the West Germans at least 400 millions. In an attempt to halt the speculation taking place in favour of their currencies, both the French and the West Germans were forced to raise their commercial banks' liquidity ratios (on which no interest rates are paid). Unfortunately, in the case of West Germany, these measures did appear to be ineffective since on Friday 14 July the *Bundesbank* had to buy up 800 million dollars and the Dutch 225 millions.

Against this atmosphere of frenzied speculation, the finance ministers met in London on 17 and 18 July, 1972 and, in principle, agreed on the following eight points. First, the new system should continue to be based on fixed, but adjustable parities. Second, it should be designed to re-establish the general convertibility of currencies. Third, there should be effective international regulation of the supply of liquidity in the world. Fourth, the new system should provide for securing necessary adjustments in the balance of payments of participating countries. Fifth, the system should have regard to the need to reduce the destabilising effects of short term capital flows. Sixth, it should conform to the principle of equal rights and obligations of all participating countries. Seventh, the new system should have special regard for the interests of the less developed countries. Eighth, such a system should not be incompatible with the progressive achievement of economic and monetary union of the enlarged EEC.

the summit meeting 19 and 20 October, 1972

The heads of state or of governments of the nine countries in the enlarged community met in Paris on 19 and 20 October. This has proven to be the most important meeting to date on the question of economic and monetary union. Foremost of the results of this summit was the reaffirmation of the desire in the community for monetary union. " The member states are determined to strengthen the community by establishing an economic and monetary union, the guarantee of stability and growth, as the foundation of their solidarity and the indispensable basis for social progress, and by ending disparities between the regions." (Contained in the communiqué of the Paris summit.) The date for completion of economic and monetary union was set at not later than 31 December, 1980.

Very few new developments took place at the Paris meeting ; the main result of the meeting was the formal consent given by all members of the enlarged community to the actions planned in the earlier meetings of March 1971 and March 1972. A fixed exchange rate system within the community continued to be viewed as a necessary basis for achieving monetary union. There is provision for the adjustment of parities but any adjustment is obviously seen as a serious wound to the achievement of monetary union. To support European currencies a European monetary co-operation fund is to be established before 1 April, 1973, to be administered by the committee of governors of central banks. The fund will be used progressively to narrow the margin of fluctuations between EEC currencies by the concerted action of central banks. Second, in order to deal with the problem of inflation in the community, there was a call for the closer co-ordination of economic policies. The eight points put forward by the meeting of finance ministers on 17 and 18 July, 1972 were again restated as being the key to " the introduction of an equitable and durable order in the international monetary system."

An extremely important feature of the summit was the stress it laid upon the creation of an effective regional policy in the EEC. The correction of regional imbalances is essential if monetary union is eventually to succeed. There was a clear direction for the setting up of a European development fund before 31 December, 1973. This is to be financed from the community's own resources (from the beginning of the second stage of economic and monetary union, which is initially timetabled for 1 January, 1974), is to work in close co-operation with national regional policies, and is to attack regional imbalances particularly created by the dependance of certain regions upon agriculture, and by industrial change and structural under employment.

TABLE IV

ANNUAL PERCENTAGE INCREASE IN CONSUMER PRICES FROM 1960 TO 1970

average increase	1960	1961	1962	1963	1964	1965	1966	1967	1968	1969	1970
in EEC countries	1.7	2.0	2.7	4.1	4.2	3.7	3.6	2.8	2.7	4.1	4.5
United Kingdom	1.0	2.9	3.8	1.9	3.3	4.7	4.0	2.5	4.7	5.4	6.4

3. implications for the United Kingdom

The over riding concern for the UK would be the implications of the process of monetary union upon her balance of payments, and upon domestic employment and economic growth. At least until the creation of a common currency in the community, even more emphasis must be placed upon balance of payments policy by the United Kingdom, and indeed by all other member countries. This will come as a result of the increasing dependence upon trade that membership would bring, and the stronger interdependence of the national economies. Without effective economic co-operation, this brings with it the increasing international transmission of national fluctuations especially in prices and employment.

payment problems would disappear

A major proportion of the national importance of the balance of payments would eventually disappear with the introduction of a common currency and a redefining of the balance of payments at the community as opposed to the national level. At such a point in time regional aid will become the main concern of each of the member states, with the United Kingdom then being one " region " within the EEC. The danger of the successive stages of monetary union is that they will progressively narrow the range of policy options available to national government to cure a payments deficit or surplus, to maintain price stability, to prevent heavy unemployment and to encourage economic growth. The initial phase of integration does not definitely exclude revaluation or devaluation of a member's currency, but such action is not to be lightly undertaken. One would suppose that in the second phase, which should begin at the latest in 1975, if recent events permit, exchange rate adjustment by member countries may be ruled out completely. It is here that one sees problems arising for the United Kingdom. In addition, fiscal harmonisation and community control over budgets, if introduced, will undoubtedly limit the flexibility of fiscal policy; that is the degree to which types and rates of taxation can be varied to influence spending throughout the nation.

The British government can, at present, seek to influence the balance of payments in two ways. It can attempt to regulate demand in the economy, through monetary and fiscal policies, in the hope that this directly affects the demand for imports, and indirectly the rate of inflation, and therefore international competitiveness. Second, it can act upon international competitiveness by attempting to control the rate of inflation by means of a prices and incomes policy, or alternatively through the alteration of the exchange rate of sterling, as in the case of the devaluation in November 1967. In the early years after entering the community it will be necessary for the United Kingdom effectively to enhance her competitiveness *vis-à-vis* the community if gains from entry are to be assured, and a favourable balance of payments position is to be maintained. This follows from a belief that by the middle of the decade the UK balance of payments will once more be in heavy deficit. A number of factors give rise to this belief. In the first place the United Kingdom is inflating at a much faster rate than most other western economies including all community members with the exception of the Netherlands (see table III above). West Germany, in particular, has had noticeable success in controlling inflation in comparison with the British performance. Taking the EEC countries together some indication can be gained from table IV (opposite) of the divergences between the EEC and British rates of inflation.

In the period from 1960 to 1970 the British rate of inflation was less than the average rate of inflation in the EEC in only four of the eleven years. If one considers the last six years the rate of inflation has fallen short of that of the EEC average in only one year. This continuing loss of competitiveness must eventually have serious repercussions upon the trade balance. Second, entry into the community will initially damage the balance of payments as it entails the loss of trade preferences in both the Commonwealth and in EFTA, and an outflow of sterling for the UK contribution to the community budget, principally to finance the CAP; in addition any increase in food prices on entry

TABLE III

PERCENTAGE INCREASE IN CONSUMER PRICES FROM 1963 TO 1970

Belgium	28.7
West Germany	20.5
Italy	28.2
France	30.9
Luxembourg	23.5
Netherlands	41.0
United Kingdom	35.3

will add to domestic inflation and stimulate further wage demands from trade unions by virtue of the subsequent increase in the cost of living. Undoubtedly, from the standpoint of the EEC, these divergencies in rates of inflation between countries present the most serious threat to the success of any system of fixed exchange rates within the community. It is apparent from the current economic climate, with approximately 3 per cent of the total work force unemployed and consumer prices increasing at a rate approaching 10 per cent per annum, that the rate of inflation in the UK is not very sensitive to changes in the level of spending in the economy. This would suggest that monetary and fiscal policies cannot alone be used to control inflation without creating heavy unemployment. Without a successful prices and incomes policy therefore, the removal of the ability of the UK to devalue the pound would prove a most serious handicap to balance of payments policy. The UK may be forced on entry into following a strong deflationary policy at a time when buoyant demand is essential and when the presumed restructuring of the economy, brought about by entry, may already be adding to frictional unemployment.

From past experience it would appear that the United Kingdom has the most to lose from a regime of fixed exchange rates throughout the community. The balance of payments objective, because of the volume of trade that takes place in the community, will continue to be the policy aim emphasised by the member countries. To maintain the competitive balance in the community it is essential that countries can work together in the co-ordination of policy so as to achieve compatible rates of inflation in all member countries. This compatibility must come about, in the absence of any other policy alternative, through domestic deflationary and reflationary policies. It is apparent in most western economies that there is an inverse relationship between the rate of change in money wages (and therefore the rate of inflation) and the level of unemployment; the higher is the level of unemployment the lower is the rate of change in money wages. The policy implications of this are that to achieve a diminution in the rate of inflation a country must reduce domestic spending and so worsen the employment situation. In comparing this "trade off" between the rate of inflation and the level of unemployment in the EEC countries and the UK, it is noticeable that the UK, in order to meet a given increase in the price level must put up with a greater level of unemployment than would be necessary in most of the EEC countries.

For example, West Germany had less than 1 per cent of its labour force unemployed in 1970, yet the rate of increase in consumer prices was less than 4 per cent in that year. Belgium, with approximately the same level of percentage unemployed as the UK in 1970, had a rate of inflation only slightly more than half that of the UK. To achieve any agreed rate of inflation in the community the UK may have to be prepared to make heavier sacrifices in terms of unemployment than most other member countries. These sacrifices will persist, in the absence of any possible adjustment of exchange rates, so long as the differences in the "trade off" between inflation and unemployment persist between member countries. Differences in this "trade off" relationship will continue until all member countries exhibit very similar identities, not only in economic fields such as in trade union structure and power, but also in the political and social fields. This will come about only when there is full integration.

Given that the UK will have to resort to deflationary/reflationary policies in the absence of exchange rate adjustment as a means of policy action, this may have serious consequences for economic growth. The effects of stop go policies upon investment and consequently growth in the 'fifties and 'sixties provided a warning against a complete reliance upon fiscal and monetary policies. The recent inflationary tendancies of the UK, far worse than anything encountered in previous years, would suggest that more severe "stop" policies may be required, with perhaps even more damaging repercussions upon growth. Furthermore, if the UK proves unable to control its inflationary bent, and our competitive position *vis-à-vis* the community is quickly worsened, the vision of "export led" growth may soon grow cloudy. It would seem a great pity that the stimulus to growth given by entry to the EEC may be partially eroded by an enforced dependance upon fiscal and monetary policies at too early a stage of monetary union.

how to minimise difficulties

An invaluable part of the initial phase of monetary union as far as the UK is concerned, is the common desire for economic co-ordination. This can be seen as an attempt to prevent the occurrence of imbalances in member countries, whether in the form of over or under employment, deficit or surplus, through economic cooperation to discuss common national economic objectives, and compatible lines of economic policy action within each national economy within the community. This becomes all the more important because of the vast inter-dependence of the national economies. In this respect the UK should adopt the approach of the "economists" in favouring economic coordination before rigidity in exchange rates is imposed within the community. On the question of the prevention of imbalances, it seems doubtful that the mobility of either labour or capital in the community could be relied upon effectively to counteract any of the forces creating imbalances in the member states. Second, particularly as far as the UK is concerned, there is a need to support currencies in times of balance of payments crises. It is imperative that the UK is not forced unnecessarily to deflate the economy simply because of pressures which may build up against sterling. This could prove very damaging to the anticipated restructuring of certain sections of the economy on entry into the EEC.

The community has brought into being short term aid for countries facing balance of payments difficulties. (A full description of this aid and its mechanics is given in appendix II.) Likewise, the community has agreed to the implementation of medium term aid. Unfortunately, this aid is likely to prove insufficient should more than one country face difficulties at any one time. Indeed, if the EEC is enlarged, larger credits would automatically have to be made available. The British delegation in Brussels would, therefore, do well if it were to put forward constructive proposals in this field. A pooling of the reserves of all the members under centralised control, with the provision of automatic aid for nations facing difficulties on current account transactions, may be one possible solution to this problem. Finally, there is the problem of maintaining sufficient policy options in order to cure possible payments, employment or growth difficulties.

The first and obvious solution to the potential British balance of payments problem is that the UK should retain the right to alter the exchange rate of the pound. Second, any deficit may be counteracted to some extent by stricter control on government expenditure abroad. The experience of the 'fifties and 'sixties would suggest that excessive government expenditure abroad was partly responsible for the problems of that period (see appendix III). On the question of fiscal harmonisation, it must be realised that the greater the degree of harmonisation introduced, the more inflexible and impotent fiscal policy becomes. This would suggest that the UK ought to support only a limited amount of fiscal harmonisation, at least until the later stages of monetary union are reached. Furthermore, harmonisation must preceed the fixity of exchange rates. Any harmonisation which takes place after the adoption of rigid exchange rates will only lead to the creation of disequilibria. Harmonisation necessarily involves differential increases or decreases in tax levels between member countries, leading to different increases or decreases in prices. This could only serve to worsen our competitive balance in the community. Again, this would constitute a criticism of the "monetarists'" approach.

Regional policy must eventually become a key feature of the community if monetary integration is to reach its ultimate conclusion, yet it has been sadly neglected in the past. It is in the development of a community regional policy that the UK may be able to contribute most to the progress towards monetary union. Albert Borschette, the member of the commission responsible for regional policy, would apparently agree with this. "I do not pretend that there is at present a coherent regional policy for the community. The council of ministers has stated that there should be one; but its elaboration remains to be completed. We shall be able to benefit in this field from the experience of the applicant countries and of the United Kingdom government in particular."

At present there is little or no effective community regional policy. The European Investment Bank has been endowed with certain aid giving powers, but between 1958 and 1970 it negotiated only $1,800 million worth of contracts, the greater proportion of which were invested in regional aid. The European Social Fund, set up under article 123 of the Rome treaty to promote "employment facilities and the geographical and occupational mobility of workers," spent only $80 million in the period from 1960 to 1968 in resettling and retraining workers in the community. Both have been most inadequate in solving the existing regional problems. As to the future, the European social fund is extending its rôle in the retraining of workers facing redundancy, the council of ministers has agreed that the agricultural fund should be used to finance the creation of new employment in the poorer farming regions, and proposals have been put forward to establish a regional development fund. It would be in the interests of the UK to support the movement towards a comprehensive regional policy in the community such that, in the event of heavy unemployment, adequate regional aid would be made available by other members of the community. This support is all the more important since the UK is not yet certain how the existing rules of the community, under article 92 of the Rome treaty, will affect its current regional policy. The industrial development certificate may, and the regional employment premium possibly will meet with opposition from other member countries, on the grounds that both represent distortions to fair competition.

The "monetarists," who seek a rapid implementation of fixed exchange rates, wish, in contrast with the old classical school of economics (which also believed in fixed exchange rates, but which used changes in the bank rates and the freedom of capital movements to bring a balance of payments back into equilibrium), to control capital movements and disequilibriating flows of "hot" money. In contrast, the "economists" wish to achieve a similar degree of economic development among member states prior to the introduction of fixed exchange rates. Also, in contrast with the "monetarists," they believe in the freedom of capital movements. Neither of these theses can be exclusively used to achieve any form of European economic and monetary integration. On the one hand, the individual member states are all at different stages of economic development (with a particularly strong industrial dominance by West Germany), and, on the other hand, the uncontrolled movement of speculative funds into western Europe has been one of the sources of inflation in the community. Also, movements of speculative funds lessen the degree of control over national *and* community monetary policy.

Apart from a whole series of safeguards and means of transforming national economies, what is needed are periodic variations in the exchange rates of the member states (to take account of changes in costs and prices) and the most severe control of monetary and capital movements. Nor does a gradual economic and monetary integration exclude the immediate creation of a European reserve unit of account. (See *European monetary integration: a* UK *appraisal,* Société Universitaire Européene de Recherches Financières, Spring 1971.) It is most important that the United Kingdom should continue to put forward constructive proposals, for the community is no "bulldozer" organisation and there exists much closer agreement between different nations on issues of concern to the United Kingdom than is often popularly imagined. (For example, between the UK and France over the control of capital movement).

the question of sterling

The problem of sterling, since the conclusion of the Basle agreements in 1968 (and their almost certain renewal in 1972) would seem to be one of popularity rather than of speculation against our currency. The term "popularity" can be easily explained by the fact that according to the terms of the Basle agreements, Britain agreed to reimburse overseas sterling holders at the then going exchange rate of $2.40 to the pound. Further, since the rates of interest in London have tended to be high, it follows that the overseas sterling holders cannot lose out; they have a gold backed guarantee at attractive rates of interest. This partly explains the rise in the overseas sterlings holdings since 1968. Should the floating of sterling lead to a fall in the popularity of our currency, this may not be a bad thing since the servicing of these holdings is not a negligible financial responsibility for Britain. Should Britain enter the common market then, she may well be presented with a golden opportunity finally to relinquish the reserve rôle of sterling, whether active or inactive. Such is the view of the French and such is the view of Harold Lever. (H. Lever, "Ending the reserve rôle of sterling:" *The Banker,* January 1971.) Harold Lever believes that these holdings make too great a call upon our balance of payments, whilst the French think that the reserve rôle of our currency confers undue privileges upon us. Certainly, the reserve rôle will not be relinquished from one day to the next, and if it is relinquished, then it will have to be done in the framework of an international organisation. Harold Lever believes it can be done by a body such as the IMF, and the latest French view (reported in *The Guardian* on 6 May, 1971) is that, if we join the community, the sterling balances should be run down over 20 years at the rate of 5 per cent a year.

The emphasis which the Segré report placed on the wealth of services offered by the London capital market, has led many people to think of London as the future capital market of an enlarged community. (*The development of a European capital market,* EEC commission, Brussels 1966.) This view deserves support, providing that this means the servicing of multi-currency loans; (according to a Bank of England statement in 1970, London is already responsible for 15 per cent of the European total). However, the temptation and danger always exist of London, in the absence of substantial balance of payments surpluses, desiring to enhance its *entrepôt* rôle by a repetition of the nineteenth century practice of borrowing short and lending long. This fear deserves to be borne in mind since the British treasury, at the end of March 1971, informed M. Boegner in Brussels, that the United Kingdom, on joining the EEC, plans to liberalise some 50 rules regarding currency and capital movements by the middle of the decade.

Until now, the moves towards the creation of a European capital market have been uncertain. Although direct investment (with certain controls still in force in the case of France) is allowed in each of the six countries, only in the case of West Germany can capital movements be said to have been freed. A long term European capital market, denominated in a European currency, was developing most strongly in 1969 but the monetary upheavals at the end of that year caused dealings to be suspended on the Frankfurt exchange and these were not resumed until March 1971. Moreover, the importance for London of the Eurodollar market (heavily dependant on the attitudes and policies of the US administration) fell considerably, in June 1970, when "regulation Q" was relaxed for large certificate deposits. As a result, large amounts of dollars flew back to the United States, indicating the danger of London's reliance on extra-European currencies over which it has no control. If, however, Britain does join the community, then she will have some influence over the rules which will be drawn up for a European capital market. She would be wise to follow the French example and exercise a great deal of caution in the drawing up of these rules, and indeed concerning an over rapid liberalisation of intra-community capital movements. One major step should be the setting up of a capital issues committee and the adoption of a common attitude towards borrowing from third parties.

Two further problems deserve attention during the initial " extended " phase of economic and monetary integration. These are the immediate question of control over borrowing from the Euro-dollar market and the proposed creation of a European capital market, which, according to the Treaty of Rome, would imply the liberalising of capital movements within the enlarged community. This latter requirement could well be implemented swiftly and discretely; it is immediately far less obvious than the much publicised Euro-dollar question, but probably potentially much more serious. Most countries in the proposed enlarged community have some form of control over short term borrowing by their nationals (individuals, firms and institutions) from the short term Euro-dollar market. In France, the controls are strict. In Britain, such borrowing was forbidden on 12 January 1971. In West Germany legislation was finally enacted in February 1972, under which short term borrowers from third parties might have to give up 40 per cent of their total borrowings in the form of liquidity ratios.

The freeing of intra-community capital movements is, due to studies currently being made in this field by the commission's committees, more imminent than is imagined. If such capital movements were freed, this could lead to the build up of excessive capital concentrations in certain centres with a possible impoverishment of others; and the danger of inflation arising in the receiving centres. Apart from the careful co-ordination of economic, fiscal and monetary policies, such a freeing of capital movements would pre-suppose the setting up of some form of capital issues committee. Should adequate precautions not be taken in time, any heavy capital outflows from countries, such as France and Britain, might lead to the adoption of deflationary policies and consequently to the evolution of even more unacceptably high levels of unemployment in both of these countries.

4. conclusions

Great importance must be attached to the extended initial transitional phase. (It may be necessary, because of the increased size of the community and the different levels of economic development between the member states to extend this phase beyond 1975.) It is essential that member states use care in preparing the ground for the next phases of integration. Should inadequate preparation lead to crises, severe disappointments may arise which might lead some members of the enlarged community to seek closer association with extra-community currencies. In order to help to achieve an orderly and relatively trouble free economic and monetary integration a detailed programme is needed. (The two authors have developed in more detail the nine point programme which they first put forward at Sussex University in February 1969, and published in "A note on monetary co-operation," P. Coffey, *Journal of common market studies,* June 1969.)

nine point programme

The basic programme for European economic and monetary integration spans the present decade. It is not possible to lay down a hard and fast timetable for integration; nevertheless, if adequate preliminary precautions are taken and if in exchange for the eventual acceptance of fixed exchange rates, those members with balance of payments surpluses are willing to place these surpluses in a common fund from which deficit countries would receive automatic help, then the enlarged community may be able to introduce a common currency (or fixed exchange rates, which amounts to the same thing) more swiftly than was first anticipated.

However, since, until such an agreement is reached and fixed exchange rates are accepted, there will continue to be a divergence between the costs and prices of goods produced in the different member states of the community, means should be found of reflecting such differences in the commercial exchange rates. Discrete and periodic agreements regarding changes in commercial exchange rates should take account of such differences.

The expression "commercial exchange rates" has been used, since there is a difference between "commercial" exchange rates, which should reflect the differences in the costs and prices of goods and services in different nations, and "financial" rates which are the rates for speculative funds. If certain controls of intra-community movements of funds, such as the setting up of a capital issues committee, are implemented, there would be no difference between "commercial" and "financial" rates. However, in the case of third parties, fixed exchange rates should be adopted (subject to periodic adjustments to reflect differences in costs and prices) for the exchange of commercial goods and services and floating rates for financial flows.

Recent experience has indicated the need for the adoption of a common attitude to third party currencies. Although in some states (notably France, Britain, the Netherlands, Italy and Switzerland) some of these forms of legislation already exist, all members should be encouraged to introduce legislation in their national parliaments enabling them, whenever necessary to forbid their nationals from borrowing on third party capital markets; to forbid the opening of non-resident deposit accounts in their commercial banks; to forbid the payment of interest on existing non-resident deposit accounts, and, where necessary, to place penal taxes on existing deposits, at least equal to any possible gains through an increase in the exchange rate of that member state; and to forbid their central banks from placing dollars on the Euro-dollar market.

In view of the grave uncertainty which surrounds the dollar, and in view of the unsatisfactory situation arising through the use, as a reserve currency, of a national currency over which the community has no control, it is important that a European unit of currency be created as a unit of reference (suggested in "A note on monetary co-operation," *op cit*). The national currencies of the EEC member states could be quoted against this unit and central banks could purchase or receive loans of this currency from a specially created European central bank.

For political and psychological reasons, it would be preferable to create a new central bank rather than use the existing Bank for International Settlements.

The successful achievement of economic and monetary integration implies the use of some degree of co-operation and self discipline among members. Already the principle of the examination of national budgets by the council of ministers before their presentation to the national parliaments has been accepted. In a similar spirit it might be desirable if the council were enabled to examine the balance of payments of member states and to make suggestions wherever heavy surpluses and/or deficits tended to be repeated. Also, in order to avoid a wastage of resources and a duplication of efforts, steps might be taken to co-ordinate the overseas aid of member states.

The successful achievement of economic and monetary integration will depend largely on whether the worn out policy of forcing states with balance of payments deficits to deflate is continued with no responsibility being placed on surplus states to inflate. In the twentieth century, it is hard to accept such a policy; such an acceptance would invalidate all the education, experiences and sacrifices of the past 50 years. Since the states of the enlarged community are embarking upon a common policy and experience, one assumes that co-operation will be necessary to enable some member states whose industries might be old fashioned and which might have made sacrifices in the field of defence, to modernise the infrastructure of their economies. Such co-operation would pre-suppose the pooling of reserves by member states. These should be pooled into a central fund which should be divided into two sections, one devoted to intra-community purposes, the other to monetary relations between the community and third parties. In the first case, member states facing balance of payments difficulties would receive automatic help from the fund. Further, the granting of automatic aid should enable fixed exchange rates to be implemented with greater ease. In the second case, the fund would be used, should the need arise, as a sort of exchange equalisation account between the currencies of the community and those of third parties.

The move towards the adoption of fixed exchange rates and the continued concentration of population in such centres as South East England and the Paris region naturally implies increasing difficulties for peripheral unfavoured regions. It is essential that a more correct balance be encouraged between the poor and the rich regions. It is, for human and economic reasons, not possible to accept the under utilisation of resources in the poor regions and the over concentration of people in the rich regions, with all the pressures on space, air and the quality of life synonymous with such influxes. A more correct balance between the two types of regions pre-supposes the creation of a regional fund endowed with considerable resources. The main responsibility of this fund should be the "declining" industrial areas in the enlarged community. The fund should work in liaison with the European investment bank (which would naturally favour infra-structure projects such as roads), and help in the modernisation and transformation of existing industries in these areas and in the implantation of new enterprises there. The fund might also take on responsibility for such payments as unemployment benefits in these areas. The international economic viability of the European Economic Community will depend on the encouragement of young but potentially important enterprises and the award of important governmental contracts to European industries. In the former case, the work of the *Institut de Développement Economique* (IDI) in France deserves attention. This independent body (using government funds) has been buying up holdings in potentially important companies, in order to help them with the financing of future investments. The creation of such an institute in the community would be of great benefit; but it must be independent and it must give funds on a community wide basis, whatever the individual national contributions to the fund may be. The encouragement of more projects like the European air bus is most desirable.

European economic and monetary integration will be an unhealthy plant if the people are not associated with the realisation of this project. The moves towards the introduction of a common currency are synonymous with the moves towards a directly elected parliament. Britain, whilst supporting this move, should give great publicity to the evolution of the accepted form of economic and monetary integration; and should also encourage the maximum contact between members of the enlarged community.

extra-community considerations

Although this paper is mainly concerned with the European Economic Community, it should not be forgotten that the two major international monetary problems at the moment are the dollar question and the problem of aid for the third world. The dollar problem has arisen because the use of the dollar as a reserve currency has conferred an exhorbitant privilege upon that currency. Thus, even where the balance of payments deficits of the United States have been caused by their excessive investments abroad (such as the buying up of European companies) and/or their military adventures in the world, western European central banks have felt obliged to buy up vast quantities of dollars which have at all times been a potential inflationary force. It is incredible that the community's central banks continue to buy up all these dollars with no possibility of reimbursement, yet were unable to support the pound sterling for only a short period of time. One must assume that the West (with the notable exception of Sweden and France) are now paying the bill for their scandalous conspiracy of silence over US crimes in Vietnam.

The European Economic Community should press for the dropping of, or a change, in clause F, article VI (2) of the statutes setting up the Special Drawing Rights, which, contrary to former IMF practice, allows the SDRS to be used to help a country experiencing deficits on capital account. Thus, all members, including the United States, would be discouraged from taking over companies in other countries. Similarly, this would be an anti-inflationary device. Then, of course, the central banks of the community should be discouraged from placing any part of their holdings on the Euro-dollar market. Equally, supporting a suggestion made at the end of last year by Pierre Mendes-France, Europeans might start buying back some of their companies from the Americans; just as we were forced to liquidate some of our holdings in America at the end of the war.

The restriction of the privileges of the major reserve currency nations will only help the third world if some form of privileges or help is expressly created for them. This might come from three sources. First, the enlarged community should adopt as progressive a policy as possible towards the developing countries. Second, in this vein, the community might adopt the French suggestion that a major part of the tariffs placed on goods coming in from the developing countries should be re-imbursed to them to help them with their own economic development. Third, when the future of the Special Drawing Rights is re-considered next year, the European Economic Community should press for the allocation of the majority of any increases to the developing countries of the world.

If the EEC were to adopt this sort of forward looking policy towards the third world soon after Britain's accession to the market, it might go some distance towards reconciling some sections of public opinion to our membership. Many socialists, especially Fabians, see the market at the moment as an inward looking institution over concerned with its only miniscule problems (such as monetary union) to the detriment of the majority of mankind and the mammoth problems of development with which they are currently wrestling. If an enlarged community were to adopt a progressive attitude towards the developing world by increasing aid and allocating to them a large proportion of SDRS, many socialists, not only in Britain but within the community itself, would view the future of the European Economic Community with much less foreboding.

5. appendices

no. I, table of plans and decisions, 1969 to 1971

1. Brussels, 12 February, 1969.

Presentation of the first Barre plan to the council of ministers.

2. The Hague, 1 and 2 December, 1969.

Communiqué issued by the conference of the heads of state.

3. Brussels, 26 January, 1970.

Acceptance by the council of finance and economic ministers of the immediate implementation of half of the Barre plan.

4. Paris, 23 and 24 February, 1970.

Presentation of the Schiller, second Barre and Giscard D'Estaing plans.

5. Venice, 29 and 30 May, 1970.

Presentation of the first Werner report to the finance ministers.

6. Luxembourg, 9 June, 1970.

Decisions by the council of ministers on the Werner report and a request for the preparation of a second report. Agreement to achieve full economic and monetary union by 1980, and not to widen the existing parity margins of EEC currencies.

7. Brussels, June 1970.

EEC commission proposal for the creation of medium term credits.

8. Brussels, 8 October, 1970.

Presentation of the second Werner report, including a suggestion to reduce the existing parity margins of EEC currencies.

9. Brussels, 14 December, 1970.

Provisional decision by the council of ministers regarding the implementation of the first stage of economic and monetary union as set out in Werner report.

10. Brussels, 9 February, 1971.

Final agreements by the council of ministers concerning the implementation of the first stage of integration,

11. Brussels, 6 and 7 March, 1972.

Basic agreements regarding narrowing of band round EEC currencies, controls over capital movements, economic co-ordination and regional policy confirmed on 21 March.

no. II, short and medium term credits

The central bankers of the six were authorised, in January 1970, to establish short term plans for monetary assistance (accomplished on 9 February, 1970). They were as follows. The provision of unconditional short term credits amounting to $1,000 million, made up of the following contributions: France $300 millions, West Germany $300 millions, Italy $200 millions, Belgium and Luxembourg $100 millions, The Netherlands $100 millions; plus the creation of a further $1,000 million of conditional short term aid (three to six months), made up in the same proportions.

How then does the agreement work in practice? The short term credits are automatic, the central bank of a member country providing the borrowing country with an amount of currency equal to the borrower's quota, in the case of West Germany, for instance, $300 million.

Allocations from the second *tranche* are made on the basis of unanimity between the central banks (the community's organs and informal committees providing the liaison). In principle, however, it was agreed that at any one particular time, only one country could draw on the full amount of the second *tranche* (minus its own quota). Thus, West Germany could draw on $1,000 million of the second *tranche* minus $300 million (her own quota) or $700 million. Since she would already be in possession of her share of the first *tranche*, however, her full drawing could amount to $1,000 million.

The commission in Brussels made a proposal regarding the creation of medium term credits for member countries experiencing balance of payments difficulties. The commission suggested that $2,000 million be provided. Loans would be made for periods of between two and five years and borrowers would have to subscribe to certain agreements regarding their national economic management. The management of this aid would be in the hands of the council of ministers (acting on the advice of the monetary committee) working on the principle of a qualified majority, on the recommendations of the commission. The council would also decide upon the duration of the loan and the rate of interest. It was suggested that this medium term aid be made up of $600 million each from France and West Germany, $400 million from Italy and $200 million each from the Netherlands and Belgium and Luxembourg together. Should a member state find itself in balance of payment difficulties as a loan operation was being made, this country would not be required to participate in the operation, but would rejoin as soon as possible after that date. In the case of a shortage of funds, the council could ask for the accelerated re-payment of debts and/or ask the help of other international organisations.

no. III, British balance of payments

During the crucial " extended " initial phase of integration, balance of payments considerations will be of paramount importance. Whilst the United Kingdom has shown a surplus on current account over the most recent years, attention should be drawn to the lesson of the 'fifties and the 'sixties when expenditure on government account overseas increased astronomically and when, on occasions, there were important capital outflows. Naturally, where government expenditure has taken the form of aid, strings are normally tied to such help. Such is not habitually the case with defence expenditure and diplomatic presence abroad. In the former case, where local labour has been employed, wage costs have substantially increased over the past decade. During the 'fifties the current account was in equilibrium but the situation was deteriorating and resulted in deficits during most of the 'sixties, with particularly severe ones in 1964 and 1965. The deterioration on current account was mainly due to two factors. First, the substantial increase in government spending abroad (in 1952 the net deficit was £62 million, and in 1965 it was £456 million). Second, the amounts earned on private services and transfers tended to fluctuate from one year to another. Taking the balance of payments as a whole, one notes fairly heavy outflows of long term capital ; in 1964 the net outflow was as high as £368 million! In the same year the net deficit on government account, together with the net outflow of long term capital, amounted to £801 million. Under such conditions it is relatively simple to imagine how any heavy deficit on the visible account would be magnified and why speculation against the pound sterling would result. Further, heavy government expenditure abroad and outflows of long term capital prevented successive British governments from building up their reserves of gold and foreign currencies to levels similar to those in EEC countries.

no. IV, narrowing EEC exchange rate margins

" The immediate suppression of the margins would entail too severe a reduction in the autonomy of control of the member states, not only in their foreign exchange relations with one another, but also in their foreign exchange relations with the outside world, which would then partake of a community nature. It would raise the supposition that the necessary conditions existed on the economic and monetary plane to ensure the hormonisation of economic policies and sufficient uniformity of rates of interest ; it would also raise the supposition that unity had been achieved on the institutional plane in the management of the foreign exchange markets of the community, and in particular that a community authority had developed that was entitled to fix the level of the dollar. For these reasons the suppression of the margins can only be contemplated at an advanced stage of the process of economic and monetary unification." (*The Werner report,* English Translation, page 45, Autumn 1970.) The committee of the governors of the central banks of the EEC were very definite in their views on the fixity of exchange rates. Complete fixity in the exchange rate relationship between EEC currencies was ruled out until a later stage in the process of monetary unification. However, it did put forward a means by which the community could move towards rigidity. This is the so called " snake in the tunnel " proposal which has since been accepted by the finance ministers of the six, and subsequently introduced.

Before the dollar crisis in May 1971 each currency was allowed to fluctuate to a level 0.75 per cent either side of its par value with the dollar, thus there was a 1.5 per cent " band " of fluctuation (the difference between the upper and lower limits of possible fluctuation in value of a currency against the dollar). As the par value of each currency was determined only against the dollar, this meant that the cross rate of any two EEC currencies could fluctuate by up to 3 per cent. This would occur, for example, when one of the currencies moved from its lower limit against the dollar to its upper limit, whilst the other currency moved from its upper limit to its lower limit against the dollar. To prevent such wide movements in exchange rates the governors of the central banks suggested that the " band " of fluctuation against the dollar should remain at 1.5 per cent over time, but at any point in time the extent by which EEC currencies would be allowed to fluctuate against each other was to be reduced to 2.4 per cent. This was to be achieved by fixing, by agreement between the member countries, a " community level " for the dollar between the band of 1.5 per cent, but not necessarily midway between the upper and lower limits of the band. At any point in time the value of any EEC currency was to be maintained within a range 0.6 per cent either side of the community level of the dollar ; although over a period of time the value of any currency could fluctuate by 0.75 per cent either side of the dollar parity (through movements in the community level of the dollar). If, for example, currency B is at the lower limit in relation to the dollar, currency A would not be allowed to go beyond a level 1.2 per cent greater than that lower limit. This effectively reduces the potential range of variation of intra-community exchange rates.

The dollar problem of 1971 prevented the introduction of such a system. However, the agreement of March 1972 called for the start, initially on an experimental basis, of a very similar exchange rate system, before 1 July, 1972. (In fact, this was introduced on 24 April, 1972.) The principle differences between this agreement and the previous proposal lie in the percentage that will be employed in relation to exchange rate margins. Since the dollar crisis the band against the dollar has been increased to 4.5 per cent ; thus the " tunnel " has become three times as wide. However, the " snake " has grown considerably fatter. Each member of the six has agreed to keep its currency at any point in time within approximately 1.12 per cent either side of the community level for the dollar, compared with the original proposal of 0.6 per cent. At the outset it appears that there are likely to be considerable pressures to reach agreement upon a community level for the dollar, particularly if some EEC currencies are weak, whilst others are strong. Those with balance of payments surpluses will be calling for a community level of the dollar above dollar parity, whilst those with deficits will be calling for a level below dollar parity to check the deficit and prevent a loss of reserves. If the agreed level is high those with surpluses may find themselves extending vast amounts of credit to support the weaker currencies in the EEC. Alternatively, it is possible that where the agreed level is low the stronger currencies will be below dollar parity, and will be accumulating reserves, and importing inflation.

table V BALANCE OF PAYMENTS, SUMMARY

£ million	1952	1953	1954	1955	1956	1957	1958
imports (free on board)	3,048	2,927	2,989	3,386	3,324	3,538	3,378
exports and re-exports (free on board)	2,769	2,683	2,785	3,073	3,377	3,509	3,407
visible balance	−279	−244	−204	−313	+ 53	− 29	+ 29
government (net): military	− 12	− 17	− 60	− 67	−101	− 61	−126
other	− 49	− 49	− 71	− 71	− 74	− 83	− 93
interest, profits and dividends (net)	+252	+229	+250	+174	+229	+249	+294
private services and transfers (net)	+251	+226	+202	+122	+101	+147	+232
invisible balance	+442	+389	+321	+158	+155	+252	+307
current balance	+163	+145	+117	−155	+208	+223	+336
official capital (net)*	− 20	− 49	− 28	− 62	− 68	+ 66	− 50
private investment (net)*	−114	−145	−163	− 60	−119	−172	−146
balance of long term capital*	−134	−194	−191	−122	−187	−106	−196
balance of current and long term capital transactions	+ 29	− 49	− 74	−277	+ 21	+117	+140
balancing item	+ 66	+ 32	+ 57	+121	+ 42	+ 90	+ 75
balance of monetary movements*	− 95	+ 17	+17	+156	− 63	−207	−215

£ million	1959	1960	1961	1962	1963	1964	1965
imports (free on board)	3,640	4,141	4,045	4,098	4,370	5,014	5,059
exports and re-exports (free on board)	3,522	3,733	3,892	3,994	4,287	4,471	4,779
visible balance	−118	−408	−153	−104	− 83	−543	−280
government (net): military	−129	−171	−199	−223	−236	−268	−276
other	− 98	−112	−134	−138	−147	−165	−180
interest, profits and dividends (net)	+267	+242	+264	+336	+396	+416	+473
private services and transfers (net)	+214	+174	+217	+230	+177	+167	+150
invisible balance	+254	+133	+148	+205	+190	+150	+176
current balance	+136	−275	− 5	+101	+107	−393	−104
official capital (net)*	−124	−103	− 45	−104	−105	−116	− 84
private investment (net)*	−131	− 89	+113	+ 6	− 65	−252	−131
balance of long term capital*	−255	−192	+ 68	− 98	−170	−368	−215
balance of current and long term capital transactions	−119	−467	+ 63	+ 3	− 63	−761	−319
balancing item	− 15	+309	− 24	+ 86	− 53	+ 27	+ 87
balance of monetary movements*	+134	+158	− 39	− 89	+116	+734	+232

**assets*: increase −/decrease+ *liabilities*: increase +/decrease−
source: Central Statistical Office, UK *balance of payments*, HMSO, 1966.

no. V, books and articles by Peter Coffey and John Presley on monetary integration in Europe

European monetary integration,	published by Macmillan, 25 November, 1971 in Britain, and by St. Martin's Press in USA.
" Monetary developments within the EEC,"	*Loughborough journal of social sciences,* November 1970.
" European monetary integration: possible consequences and solutions,"	*Loughborough journal of social sciences,* November 1970.
" European monetary integration: implications for the UK,"	*National Westminster Bank review,* February 1971.
The European monetary problem,	European society of financial research, Spring 1971.
" London and the development of a European capital market,"	*The bankers' magazine,* June 1971.
" European monetary integration,"	*Clare market review,* Summer 1971.
" On exchange rate unification: a comment in relation to the EEC,"	*Economic journal,* December 1972.
" The European capital market,"	in *Euromoney,* November 1971.
" A note on monetary co-operation,"	*Journal of common market studies,* June 1969.